Healing in His Wings

Healing in His Wings

CAROLYN RHEA

BROADMAN PRESS

Nashville, Tennessee

4251-50
ISBN: 0-8054-5150-1

Dewey Decimal Classification: 242.4
Subject Headings: CONSOLATION/ /MEDITATIONS

Library of Congress Catalog Card Number: 68-31348
Printed in the United States of America

*Carolyn Rhea of Birmingham, Alabama, is the author of
several books by Broadman and other publishers. She is a
teacher and also fills many speaking engagements. Her
husband, Claude, is dean of the School of Music at Samford
University.*

Dedicated
to
those who have also journeyed
in the caravan
of
pain and sorrow

Foreword

In this little book I have conversed with those who "visited" me at times of physical illness and earthly sorrow. Imagined dialogue with both Bible characters and intangible qualities of the spirit are all intermingled in an effort to grow toward spiritual maturity through the experience of pain and sorrow.

You are invited to listen in, for perhaps they have visited you too.

The struggle is not over. My pilgrimage toward spiritual maturity continues.

Contents

———•••———

. . . Unto you that fear my name shall the Sun of righteousness arise with healing in his wings; and ye shall go forth, and grow up . . .

MALACHI 4:2

Elijah

———————

Elijah, let us visit for a while!
You—under your juniper
And I beneath my weeping willow.

You understand then,
This utter self-pity
And sense of desolation?

Am I forsaken—all alone?
Not so? You say
That God is near
And others have journeyed this very way?
The tree is for a moment's rest
In our human desert of despair
But God's oasis lies ahead
For those who bravely
Join His caravan?

Come, then, let us move on.

HEALING IN HIS WINGS . . .

But unto you that fear my name shall the Sun of right-eousness arise with healing in his wings; and ye shall go forth and grow up. MALACHI 4:2a

But he himself went a day's journey into the wilder-ness, and came and sat down under a juniper tree: and he requested for himself that he might die. . . . The word of the Lord came to him, and he said unto him, What doest thou here, Elijah? And he said, Go forth.
1 KINGS 19:4a,9b,11a

For I am poor and needy, and my heart is wounded within me. Help me, O Lord my God.
PSALM 109:22,26a

The Lord shall give thee rest from thy sorrow.
ISAIAH 14:3b

They that wait upon the Lord shall renew their strength; they shall mount up with wings as eagles; they shall run, and not be weary; and they shall walk, and not faint. ISAIAH 40:31

Illness

———•◆•———

Illness, you ugly parasite!
Like mistletoe, you've entrenched yourself upon my
    body!
As you bloom and grow, you feed upon my strength.

I shall fight!
Battalions stand by to help!
My doctor's scalpel will sever you.
Modern medicine will shrivel you.
You shall fall to the ground,
And I shall stand again strong and well.

But what if I cannot conquer you?
If you are with me still
As my constant, inevitable companion,
I pray that God will help me
Learn to live with you in peace
And somehow discover how you, my enemy—
Like mistletoe at Christmas—
Can serve some useful purpose.

HEALING IN HIS WINGS . . .

Consider mine affliction and deliver me: for I do not forget thy law. PSALM 119:153

Who healeth all thy diseases. PSALM 103:3b

But watch thou in all things, endure afflictions.

2 TIM. 4:5a

The spirit of a man will sustain his infirmity.

PROV. 18:14a

Give us help from trouble: for vain is the help of man.
   Through God we shall do valiantly: for he it is that shall tread down our enemies. PSALM 108:12,13

Though our outward man perish, yet the inward man is renewed day by day. 2 COR. 4:16b

It is good for me that I have been afflicted; that I might learn thy statutes. PSALM 119:71

Come unto me, all ye that labour and are heavy laden, and I will give you rest. Take my yoke upon you, and learn of me; for I am meek and lowly in heart: and ye shall find rest unto your souls. For my yoke is easy, and my burden is light. MATT. 11:28–30

Miriam

Miriam, how can you be so gay
With timbrel in your hand
When it's winter in my heart?

Grief has numbed my senses
And I'm in hibernation.

You say that time will pass
And warmth of spring
Will thaw the cold
And stir up joy once more
And I shall laugh again?

HEALING IN HIS WINGS . . .

My harp also is tuned to mourning, and my organ into the voice of them that weep. JOB 30:31

Ye shall weep and lament, but the world shall rejoice; and ye shall be sorrowful, but your sorrow shall be turned into joy. JOHN 16:20b

Because thou shalt forget thy misery, and remember it as waters that pass away. JOB 11:16

I will turn their mourning into joy, and will comfort them. JER. 31:13b

Weeping may endure for a night, but joy cometh in the morning. PSALM 30:5b

The hope of the righteous shall be gladness.

PROV. 10:28a

The Lord hath done great things for us; whereof we are glad.
They that sow in tears shall reap in joy.

PSALM 126:3,5

Blessed are ye that weep now: for ye shall laugh.

LUKE 6:21

[15]

Jonah

<hr />

Jonah, I'm trapped too
Inside the whale of circumstance!
There is no visible escape and
In the darkness I cry out to God
Imploring His mercy and a second opportunity.

You say there is a way out
If we but find His door?
That if we abide more closely in His presence
Our eyes become adjusted
And we can see the latch which opens it.
Because of this encounter, then,
I shall emerge like you, Jonah, with new purpose and
    direction.

HEALING IN HIS WINGS . . .

———— •◆•◆• ————

*Then Jonah prayed unto the Lord his God out of the
fish's belly.*

*And the Lord spake unto the fish, and it vomited out
Jonah upon the dry land.*

And Jonah arose and went unto Nineveh.

JONAH 2:1,10;3:3a

*But God is faithful, who will not suffer you to be
tempted above that ye are able; but will with the temp-
tation also make a way to escape, that ye may be able
to bear it. 1 COR. 10:13b*

*We are troubled on every side, yet not distressed; we
are perplexed, but not in despair.*

*Persecuted, but not forsaken; cast down, but not
destroyed. 2 COR. 4:8,9*

Thou feedest them with the bread of tears.

PSALM 80:5a

*After that ye have suffered awhile, make you perfect,
stablish, strengthen, settle you. 1 PETER 5:10b*

[17]

Joseph

———•••———

Joseph, man of dreams
Interpret mine for me.

If I but close my eyes
Nightmares I see
    Of fears
      Of sins
        Of neglected opportunity.

You say these point up
Spiritual famine?

But then you say that God
Who sees ahead
Has made provision for it
And if I but draw from His great store of love
My hunger will be fed
And I shall lie down
To pleasant dreams.

HEALING IN HIS WINGS . . .

Thou shalt not be afraid for the terror by night.

PSALM 91:5a

When thou liest down, thou shalt not be afraid: yea, thou shalt lie down, and thy sleep shall be sweet.

PROV. 3:24

I will both lay me down in peace, and sleep: for thou, Lord, only makest me dwell in safety. PSALM 4:8

For he satisfieth the longing soul, and filleth the hungry soul with goodness. PSALM 107:9

Cast thy burden upon the Lord, and he shall sustain thee. PSALM 55:22a

Then they cry unto the Lord in their trouble, and he bringeth them out of their distresses.

He maketh the storm a calm, so that the waves thereof are still.

Then are they glad because they be quiet; so he bringeth them unto their desired haven.

PSALM 107:28–30

Rest in the Lord, and wait patiently for him.

PSALM 37:7a

Come unto me, all ye that labour and are heavy laden, and I will give you rest. MATT. 11:28

[19]

Despair

Despair, like unhealthy smog
You have engulfed me
And weakened all my senses.

I cannot see the way ahead
To avoid the pitfalls, the collisions,
And pursue the right direction.
I stagger. I stumble all alone.
This pollution smothers me.

He who is above, beyond the smog of Earth
Sees clearly all the way
So I, in trust, shall place my hand in His.
He'll lead me safely through.

Healing in His Wings . . .

Out of the depths have I cried unto thee, O Lord.
PSALM 130:1

I complained, and my spirit was overwhelmed.
PSALM 77:3b

I stretch forth my hands unto thee. PSALM 143:6a

Cause me to hear thy lovingkindness in the morning; for in thee do I trust: cause me to know the way wherein I should walk; for I lift up my soul unto thee.
PSALM 143:8

For thou wilt light my candle: the Lord my God will enlighten my darkness. PSALM 18:28

When by his light I walked through darkness.
JOB 29:3b

Fear

———•◆•———

Fear! Where did you come from?
It's night. All guests are gone,
And I must rest.

Have you been lurking in the closet
Waiting for darkness, when like
Some rabid bat you can swoop out and attack?

You dare defend yourself!
You say you're not aggressive—just impersonal—
A useful part in God's provision for defense?
That you are more like a rope in my hands
Which I can learn to handle?
That if I panic and struggle,
I could tie myself up helplessly;
But, if I let Him, God can teach me
How to tie successive knots
And use you as a ladder
To climb to higher ground.

[22]

HEALING IN HIS WINGS . . .

————•◆••————

Be not afraid of sudden fear . . .
  For the Lord shall be thy confidence.

PROV. 3:25a,26a

What time I am afraid, I will trust in thee. PSALM 56:3

*I sought the Lord, and he heard me, and delivered me
from all my fears.* PSALM 34:4

*I can do all things through Christ which strengtheneth
me.* PHIL. 4:13

*God hath not given us the spirit of fear; but of power,
and of love, and of a sound mind.* 2 TIM. 1:7

*The Lord is my helper, and I will not fear what man
shall do unto me.* HEB. 13:6b

Perfect love casteth out fear. 1 JOHN 4:18b

Courage

Courage, come sit awhile with me.

You are the evergreen of life
Whose lovely leaves stay bright and bold
Even in the fiercest winter storm.

Why can't I be like you?
Once my leaves were green and fresh
But in these changing seasons
Of sickness and distress
They have turned an ugly brown
Dropped from me to the ground;
And now I stand alone,
Vulnerable to the world.

But you say it's not the leaves
That matter most?
That my trunk and limbs still bravely stand
And bright green leaves can grow again?

Then Courage is not just shining leaves
But the inner resources
Which help the tree to stand
Through every season.

Courage, come stand by me.

[24]

HEALING IN HIS WINGS . . .

And the rain descended, and the floods came, and the winds blew, and beat upon that house; and it fell not: for it was founded upon a rock. MATT. 7:25

And having done all, to stand. EPHES. 6:13b

Behold, we count them happy which endure.
JAMES 5:11a

Be strong and of good courage. DEUT. 31:6a

Strengthen ye the weak hands, and confirm the feeble knees. ISAIAH 35:3

Be of good courage, and let us behave ourselves valiantly. 1 CHRON. 19:13a

Watch ye, stand fast in the faith, quit you like men, be strong. 1 COR. 16:13

I can do all things through Christ which strengtheneth me. PHIL. 4:13

Patience

———•—•—

Patience, your easy manner
Soothes my sore distress
And calms my frantic pace.
If you would but sit with me
Each day and night
I would not hurt myself or others so.

You say you have been near always?
That it was I who turned away from You?
O yes, I do recall seeing you briefly by my side,
But tossed about with pain and weariness,
I simply turned my face to the wall;
And rebelliously tangled up inside,
I screamed and kicked and sobbed.

I must be still inside and out
And let your gentle hand
Help comb the tangles out each day.

HEALING IN HIS WINGS . . .

Patient in tribulation. ROM. 12:12b

Ye have need of patience. HEB. 10:36a

Knowing this, that the trying of your faith worketh patience.
But let patience have her perfect work, that ye may be perfect and entire, wanting nothing. JAMES 1:3,4

Let us run with patience the race that is set before us,
Looking unto Jesus the author and finisher of our faith. HEB. 12:1b,2a

Follow after righteousness, godliness, faith, love, patience, meekness. I TIM. 6:11b

And beside this, giving all diligence, add to your faith virtue; and to virtue knowledge; and to temperance patience. II PET. 1:5,6b

In your patience possess ye your souls. LUKE 21:19

Faith

Stand tall beside me, Faith!
You are the spiritual antenna
Which tunes me in to God.
Though now I fear
This monument of grief
Towers so painfully close
That it obstructs the path of clear reception between
    my God and me,
And static of doubt interferes.

Yet I know that He is near
And that you, Faith, reveal His compassionate concern
    for me, His child.

So reach skyward, Faith!
Higher still!
Reach out above this towering grief
And bring in clearly
The reassuring message of God's enduring love and
    His sustaining help
During this difficult experience.

Healing in His Wings . . .

———————

If ye have faith, and doubt not . . . MATT. 21:21b

And the apostles said unto the Lord, Increase our faith.
LUKE 17:5

*For therein is the righteousness of God revealed from
faith to faith: as it is written, The just shall live by
faith.* ROM. 1:17

*Above all, taking the shield of faith, wherewith ye shall
be able to quench all the fiery darts of the wicked.*
EPHES. 6:16

*Let us draw near with a true heart in full assurance of
faith.* HEB. 10:22a

*But without faith it is impossible to please him: for he
that cometh to God must believe that he is, and that
he is a rewarder of them that diligently seek him.*
HEB. 11:6

*Therefore being justified by faith, we have peace
with God through our Lord Jesus Christ:*
*By whom also we have access by faith unto this
grace wherein we stand, and rejoice in hope of the glory
of God.* ROM. 5:1,2

[29]

Eve

———•◆•◆•———

Eve, I feel so condescending toward you.
You've been my whipping post
Through all these years.
I scorn your weakness in yielding to sin,
Thus causing me to fall.
You deserve the blame.

You say you understand my condemnation?
That you'd like so much to start again
And circumvent that awful sin?
You say also that I must grow up in accepting my own
    responsibility?
That I have done no better,
And my own fresh page of history
Is marred also?

Praise God, there is a difference!
For Christ has come between the "then" and "now"
And there is healing and forgiveness in His wings.

HEALING IN HIS WINGS . . .

But I fear, lest by any means, as the serpent beguiled Eve through his subtilty, so your minds should be corrupted from the simplicity that is in Christ.

2 COR. 11:3

If I justify myself, mine own mouth shall condemn me.

JOB 9:20a

And why beholdest thou the mote that is in thy brother's eye, but considerest not the beam that is in thine own eye? MATT. 7:3

Wherein thou judgest another, thou condemnest thyself; for thou that judgest doest the same things.

ROM. 2:1b

So then every one of us shall give account of himself to God. ROM. 14:12

For as in Adam all die, even so in Christ shall all be made alive. 1 COR. 15:22

Hope

———

Hope, you're such a cheerful friend!
Your visits warm and bless,
And your optimism is quite contagious!

You're the lovely Easter egg
I so gaily decorate
With bright, gay colors of health and happiness
And then hide in some secret place.

Perhaps someday I shall find you again in reality
And tuck you happily into the basket of my life.

But even if I should not find you again
I've had the joy of
Playing with you now.

HEALING IN HIS WINGS . . .

The hope of the righteous shall be gladness.

PROV. 10:28

Therefore my heart is glad, and my glory rejoiceth: my flesh also shall rest in hope. PSALM 16:9

Why art thou cast down, O my soul? and why art thou disquieted within me? hope in God. PSALM 43:5a

The God of hope fill you with all joy and peace in believing, that ye may abound in hope. ROM. 15:13a

Now abideth . . . hope . . . 1 COR. 13:13a

Which hope we have as an anchor of the soul, both sure and steadfast. HEB. 6:19a

And thou shalt be secure, because there is hope.

JOB 11:18a

David

David, bring your harp and sing.
Help me forget my woes
And be a trusting child again.

Sing to me of courage
God's power to use a simple sling
To slay all threatening giants.

Sing to me of faith
To trust Him in the dark
Believing light will surely shine again.

Sing of God's forgiveness
Even for the darkest sins
His power to cleanse and make me whole again.

HEALING IN HIS WINGS . . .

———•••———

Restore unto me the joy of thy salvation; and uphold me with thy free spirit. PSALM 51:12

Have mercy upon me, O God, according to thy loving-kindness: according unto the multitude of thy tender mercies blot out my transgressions. PSALM 51:1

But I am like a green olive tree in the house of God: I trust in the mercy of God forever and ever.

PSALM 52:8

Yea, in the shadow of thy wings will I make my refuge, until these calamities be overpast. PSALM 57:1b

Because thou hast been my help, therefore in the shadow of thy wings will I rejoice. PSALM 63:7

Keep me as the apple of the eye, hide me under the shadow of thy wings. PSALM 17:8

Martha

Martha, come sympathize with me!
You know, as I,
There's so much work
And I must do my part!
Just think of all the tasks
That are accumulating
As I idly lie abed
Unable to lift a hand!

You say that others can carry on
Life's essentials?
That I, like you, kept adding trifles day by day
When I should have been subtracting them instead
So I could multiply my time with God.

There are no trifles now to interfere
And there is time
To sit quietly at the Master's feet
And learn the lessons
I've been missing all along.

[36]

Healing in His Wings . . .

———•◆•———

But Martha was cumbered about much serving, and came to him, and said, Lord, dost thou not care that my sister hath left me to serve alone? bid her therefore that she help me.

And Jesus answered and said unto her, Martha, Martha, thou art careful and troubled about many things:

But one thing is needful: and Mary hath chosen that good part, which shall not be taken away from her.

Luke 10:40–42

But seek ye first the kingdom of God, and his righteousness; and all these things shall be added unto you.

Matt. 6:33

Study to show thyself approved unto God, a workman that needeth not to be ashamed. II Tim. 2:15a

Teach me thy way, O Lord. Psalm 27:11a

. . . Learn of me; for I am meek and lowly in heart: and ye shall find rest unto your souls. Matt. 11:29b

Paul

Welcome, Paul, for you too have traveled
This path before.
You understand
The constant prick of pain upon one's flesh.

Is there no relief, no surcease,
No joy in life?
How can I endure?

You say I *can't!*
Not in my strength alone?
But that His strength has proved
Sufficient day by day?
The trusting soul still sees life's roses
And a cheerful heart
Enjoys their fragrance
In spite of thorny pricks of pain.

HEALING IN HIS WINGS . . .

And lest I should be exalted above measure through the abundance of the revelations, there was given to me a thorn in the flesh, the messenger of Satan to buffet me, lest I should be exalted above measure.

For this thing I besought the Lord thrice, that it might depart from me.

And he said unto me, My grace is sufficient for thee: for my strength is made perfect in weakness. Most gladly therefore will I rather glory in my infirmities, that the power of Christ may rest upon me.

2 COR. 12:7–9

O bring thou me out of my distresses. Look upon mine affliction and my pain. PSALM 25:17b,18a

Who shall separate us from the love of Christ? shall tribulation, or distress, or persecution?

Nay, in all these things we are more than conquerors through him that loved us. ROM. 8:35a,37

Boaz

Boaz, did duty drive you
To shoulder your responsibility
To Ruth, your kin?

You say you discovered that love makes duty, pleasure?

Responsibilities, then, cannot be hammered out on the
     harsh anvil of duty alone.
They must first be softened in the blaze of Love.

HEALING IN HIS WINGS . . .

———•—•—•———

Love is the fulfilling of the law. ROM. 13:10b

Owe no man anything, but to love one another: for he that loveth another hath fulfilled the law. ROM. 13:8

By love serve one another. GAL. 5:13b

Let us not love in word, neither in tongue; but in deed and in truth. I JOHN 3:18b

God is not unrighteous to forget your work and labour of love, which ye have shewed toward his name, in that ye have ministered to the saints, and do minister.

HEB. 6:10

Inasmuch as ye have done it unto one of the least of these my brethren, ye have done it unto me.

MATT. 25:40b

Death

———•━••━•———

Death, you Villain!
Rob me of life—my ready cash?
Destroy this body—my earthly purse which holds it?
How dare you!
I shall defend myself
And lock in deadly duel!
But if you should triumph at last
You cannot rob me of my greatest wealth—my true
    identity—my Self,
Safely deposited with God.

Behind the scenes, back in the wings
When our disguise is shed
And masks are put away
I think I shall discover, Death, that only in
    life's final act
Your role seemed that of Villain;
And in the full drama of eternity
Perhaps I shall know you as a Friend.

HEALING IN HIS WINGS . . .

Yea, though I walk through the valley of the shadow of death, I will fear no evil: for thou art with me; thy rod and thy staff they comfort me. PSALM 23:4

Fear not them which kill the body, but are not able to kill the soul. MATT. 10:28a

Into thine hand I commit my spirit: thou hast redeemed me, O Lord God of truth. PSALM 31:5

If in this life only we have hope in Christ, we are of all men most miserable. I COR. 15:19

But God will redeem my soul from the power of the grave: for he shall receive me. PSALM 49:15

The righteous hath hope in his death. PROV. 14:32b

[43]

Job

————•—•—•————

Job, how thrilling to have heard God's mighty voice!
Oh, that I might seek and find Him too!

I live in such noise and clamor
That it would take His whirlwind trumpet call
To be heard above it.

God does not always speak that way?
You say that His approach does not break our sound
    barriers?
That He comes quietly but surely, too?
Then I must tune my ears
To hear His higher pitch.

[44]

HEALING IN HIS WINGS . . .

Then the Lord answered Job out of the whirlwind.

JOB 38:1a

And, behold, the Lord passed by, and a great and strong wind rent the mountains, and brake in pieces the rocks before the Lord; but the Lord was not in the wind: and after the wind an earthquake; but the Lord was not in the earthquake:

And after the earthquake a fire; but the Lord was not in the fire: and after the fire a still small voice.

I KINGS 19:11b,12

Be still, and know that I am God: I will be exalted among the heathen, I will be exalted in the earth.

PSALM 46:10

Hearken unto this, O Job: stand still, and consider the wondrous works of God. JOB 37:14

He that hath ears to hear, let him hear. MATT. 11:15

[45]

Anger

———•—•—•———

Anger, you're here again!
I feel guilty in your presence,
Ashamed of even knowing you.

You claim to be a friend—but how?
You say it's natural to have some angry feelings?
That it's somewhat like carbon dioxide in breathing?
Formed inside, you must be breathed out again
Lest your overcrowded presence leave no room
For the continuous inflow of oxygen—
Those good feelings of love and compassion
So necessary for a healthy, growing life?

As I mature then, and better understand your role
I must learn to channel you into healthy outlets which
    do not injure others?

Even as there are constructive uses for carbon dioxide
You too, Anger, when you are truly Righteous Indigna-
    tion,
Can help to work for good on Earth.

Healing in His Wings . . .

Be ye angry, and sin not: let not the sun go down upon your wrath. Eph. 4:26

Let all bitterness, and wrath, and anger, and clamour, and evil speaking, be put away from you, with all malice. Eph. 4:31

He that is slow to anger is better than the mighty; and he that ruleth his spirit than he that taketh a city.
Prov. 16:32

A soft answer turneth away wrath: but grievous words stir up anger. Prov. 15:1

And Jesus went into the temple of God, and cast out all them that sold and bought in the temple, and overthrew the tables of the moneychangers, and the seats of them that sold doves. Matt. 21:12

[47]

Forgiveness

Forgiveness, draw nearer, please.
I felt no need of you before,
But now I know you are my greatest need.

Sin is a festering sore within my body.
My home remedies failed to cure,
And desperately I have covered it with an awkward
bandage
To hide it from my view and others.
Now I've discovered the tape has adhered to it.

I must endure the pain of exposing it openly and
honestly
To myself and Christ
And humbly ask Him, the Great Physician,
To direct you, Forgiveness, His healing laser beam,
upon it.

You say I too must use you
In my relationship with others
And must direct your healing beam
Upon their trespasses against me?

[48]

HEALING IN HIS WINGS . . .

He that covereth his sins shall not prosper: but whoso confesseth and forsaketh them shall have mercy.

PROV. 28:13

I said, Lord, be merciful unto me: heal my soul; for I have sinned against thee. PSALM 41:4

O God, thou knowest my foolishness; and my sins are not hid from thee. PSALM 69:5

If we confess our sins, he is faithful and just to forgive us our sins, and to cleanse us from all unrighteousness.

1 JOHN 1:9

And forgive us our debts, as we forgive our debtors.

MATT. 6:12

For if ye forgive men their trespasses, your heavenly Father will also forgive you. MATT. 6:14

Forgive, and ye shall be forgiven. LUKE 6:37b

[49]

Prayer

———•••———

Prayer, you are the God-given prism I hold in my hand
With power to refract or bend
God's healing love
Into the deep recesses of my soul.

You separate the single beam of
His love into a multicolor
Spectrum of manifested care.
You reflect the image of Him
Who loves, Who cares,
     Heals,
       Forgives,
         Sustains.

Prayer, you are a marvelous Friend!

Healing in His Wings . . .

———•◆•———

Is any among you afflicted? let him pray. James 5:13a

The effectual fervent prayer of a righteous man availeth much. James 5:16b

The Lord is nigh unto all them that call upon him, to all that call him in truth. Psalm 145:18

And all things, whatsoever ye shall ask in prayer, believing, ye shall receive. Matt. 21:22

If ye abide in me, and my words abide in you, ye shall ask what ye will, and it shall be done unto you.
                                             John 15:7

I will pray with the spirit, and I will pray with the understanding also. 1 Cor. 14:15a

And this is the confidence that we have in him, that, if we ask anything according to his will, he heareth us.
                                             1 John 5:14

Security

So you have words for me,
O crippled man of Bethesda?

You ask me, even as Christ asked you beside the pool
that day,
"Do you really *want* to be well?
Then take up your bed and walk."

Lord Jesus, forgive my childish ways.
Pry these tightly clutched fingers
From my dirty little "security blanket" of worldly
riches.
Wean me from the compulsive thumb sucking pleasure
of earthly success,
And let me not crawl through life hugging earth's floor.

I look up to Thee, O Lord,
For I truly *want* to stand and walk on growing legs of
faith,
Unhampered by childish "*in*securities."

For Thy love for me
And my faith and trust in Thee
Are my only real security.

[52]

HEALING IN HIS WINGS . . .

When I was a child, I spake as a child, I understood as a child, I thought as a child: but when I became a man, I put away childish things. 1 COR. 13:11

Set your affection on things above, not on things on the earth. COL. 3:2

Seek ye first the kingdom of God, and his righteousness; and all these things shall be added unto you.
MATT. 6:33

For I am persuaded, that neither death, nor life, nor angels, nor principalities, nor powers, nor things present, nor things to come,
Nor height, nor depth, nor any other creature, shall be able to separate us from the love of God, which is in Christ Jesus our Lord. ROM. 8:38,39

For I know whom I have believed, and am persuaded that he is able to keep that which I have committed unto him against that day. 2 TIM. 1:12b

Words

————◦•◦————

Words, as if from a leaking faucet
You drip endlessly
From my tongue each day.
Sharp, unkind, impatient ones
And endless chatter.

Forgive this waste of words, O Lord.
Tighten my control,
That from my lips might flow
Gentle words and kind
To water thirsty lives;
And if no words are needed, Lord,
Please help me turn the faucet off.

Healing in His Wings . . .

———◆◆◆———

The words of a man's mouth are as deep waters, and the wellspring of wisdom as a flowing brook. Prov. 18:4

A continual dropping in a very rainy day and a contentious woman are alike. Prov. 27:15

The lips of the righteous feed many. Prov. 10:21a

A wholesome tongue is a tree of life. Prov. 15:4a

Let the words of my mouth, and the meditation of my heart, be acceptable in thy sight, O Lord, my strength and my redeemer. Psalm 19:14

Be thou an example of the believers, in word, in conversation . . . 1 Tim. 4:12b

The tongue of the just is as choice silver. Prov. 10:20a

Love

———•◦•◦•———

Love, dear friend,
You're with me still;
For I'm aware of your presence.

You're the fertile soil deep inside
In which I've grown
Rich, rewarding relationships
Through the years.

Those seeds I planted
In sandy soil too near the surface
Did not survive;
But those relationships
Which I planted deep within you, Love,
Were nourished faithfully;
And healthy, growing roots
Enabled them to reach maturity and bear fruit.

Love, you've made me rich indeed.

HEALING IN HIS WINGS . . .

The Lord make you to increase and abound in love one toward another, and toward all men. I THES. 3:12a

My little children, let us not love in word, neither in tongue; but in deed and in truth. I JOHN 3:18

If we love one another, God dwelleth in us, and his love is perfected in us. I JOHN 4:12b

Keep yourselves in the love of God. JUDE 1:21

Charity (love) suffereth long, and is kind; charity envieth not; charity vaunteth not itself, is not puffed up.
Beareth all things, believeth all things, hopeth all things, endureth all things. I COR. 13:4,7

Regrets

———·•••·———

Regrets, you are the smudges on the pages of my
    life . . .
The holes so childishly dug trying to erase mis-
    takes . . .
The misspelled words . . .
The punctuation omitted or misplaced . . .
The big words so glibly but wrongly used before ex-
    periencing their true meaning.
How I'd like to change you, but that can never be;
For life is a rough draft essay handed in to God each
    day.
I can re-read, but I cannot re-write.

The lessons I learn today, though,
Can be evidenced in tomorrow's page.

HEALING IN HIS WINGS . . .

Who is this that darkeneth counsel by words without knowledge? JOB 38:2

Therefore have I uttered that I understood not; things too wonderful for me, which I knew not.
I have heard of thee by the hearing of the ear: but now mine eye seeth thee. Wherefore I abhor myself, and repent in dust and ashes. JOB 42:3b,5,6

Hide thy face from my sins, and blot out all mine iniquities. Create in me a clean heart, O God; and renew a right spirit within me. PSALM 51:9,10

By mercy and truth iniquity is purged: and by the fear of the Lord men depart from evil. PROV. 16:6

When pride cometh, then cometh shame: but with the lowly is wisdom. PROV. 11:2

Abraham

Abraham, how did you do it!
How could you leave all that was dear and familiar
And journey bravely into the unknown?

I find it so hard to move
From one circumstance to another—
From health to sickness,
From happiness to sorrow,
From the familiar to the unknown.

God meets you there, you say?
He has gone before and prepared for you?

Make me ready, Lord, each time that I must move
From one circumstance to another.
Strengthen my faith that You have prepared for me at
    my next destination.
Help me discard the clutter as I go along
And take only eternal treasures and necessity.

And when my last move is Earth to Heaven,
Help me face it with the calm assurance
That you have prepared the way.

HEALING IN HIS WINGS . . .

How shall we sing the Lord's song in a strange land?
PSALM 137:4

By faith Abraham, when he was called to go out into a place which he should after receive for an inheritance, obeyed; and he went out, not knowing whither he went.
HEB. 11:8

The Lord shall preserve thy going out and thy coming in from this time forth, and even forevermore.
PSALM 121:8

And he brought forth his people with joy, and his chosen with gladness. PSALM 105:43

In my Father's house are many mansions: if it were not so, I would have told you. I go to prepare a place for you. And if I go and prepare a place for you, I will come again, and receive you unto myself; that where I am, there ye may be also. JOHN 14:2,3

[61]

Peter

Oh, Peter, you're such a rock
And I'm just sinking sand!

You say there's hope?
That one becomes a rock
In different ways?

Sudden, volcanic tragedy in one's life
Can cool and solidify into igneous rock?
Or steady drippings
Of heartache and despair evaporate
And the deposits which they leave
Form sedimentary rock?

I see, then, it is
God who transforms
The weak and wavering self
Into solid metamorphic rock
If we but let Him.

HEALING IN HIS WINGS . . .

Finally, my brethren, be strong in the Lord, and in the power of his might. EPH. 6:10

I can do all things through Christ which strengtheneth me. PHIL. 4:13

Nay, in all these things we are more than conquerors through him that loved us. ROM. 8:37

He giveth power to the faint; and to them that have no might he increaseth strength. ISA. 40:29

Blessed is the man whose strength is in thee.

PSALM 84:5a

The God of all grace, who hath called us unto his eternal glory by Christ Jesus, after that ye have suffered a while, make you perfect, stablish, strengthen, settle you. 1 PET. 5:10

Influence

Influence, I cannot seem to shake you!
Like a quiet shadow
You go in and out with me.
Someone has said that you're my "personality fall-out."

Why can't I be alone in this my hour of grief
And not be held accountable
For the way I handle it?

You say that we're inseparable
Linked together still
That though I close off the world from *me*
No doors can hide you from their view?

That as I walk the perimeter of my life each day
My steps merely trace its outline
And add up only the distance around.
While you, my Influence, are the multiplied part of *me*
Which, falling out,
Has covered all the area inside.

Healing in His Wings . . .

Ye are our epistle written in our hearts, known and read of all men:

Forasmuch as ye are manifestly declared to be the epistle of Christ . . .

2 Cor. 3:2,3a

Let your light so shine before men, that they may see your good works, and glorify your Father which is in heaven.

Matt. 5:16

Be thou an example of the believers, in word, in conversation, in charity, in spirit, in faith, in purity.

1 Tim. 4:12b

And makest manifest the savour of his knowledge by us in every place. For we are unto God a sweet savour of Christ, in them that are saved, and in them that perish.

2 Cor. 2:14b,15

. . . Lest I make my brother to offend.

1 Cor. 8:13b

Zaccheus

Zaccheus, were you burdened with finances too?
Did obligations overwhelm
And drive you to such a despicable livelihood?

You say Christ taught you much
Those few moments in your home
And straightened out your ledger?
Assured us He would give strength and opportunity
To help us meet our needs
If our greater values were in their rightful place?

Then I shall close my unbalanced books,
Lock worry outside,
And rest confidently in Him.

HEALING IN HIS WINGS . . .

———— ◆ ————

But seek ye first the kingdom of God, and his righteousness; and all these things shall be added unto you.

MATT. 6:33

So is he that layeth up treasure for himself, and is not rich toward God.

LUKE 12:21

Rest in the Lord, and wait patiently for him.

PSALM 37:7a

A man's life consisteth not in the abundance of the things which he possesseth.

LUKE 12:15b

For where your treasure is, there will your heart be also.

MATT. 6:21

Charge them that are rich in this world, that they be not highminded, nor trust in uncertain riches, but in the living God, who giveth us richly all things to enjoy.

1 TIM. 6:17

There is that maketh himself rich, yet hath nothing; there is that maketh himself poor, yet hath great riches.

PROV. 13:7

Kindness

———•◦•◦•———

Kindness, you're the seasonal filter
For life's conditioning.

In my heat of anger
You've tried to trap the lint and dirt
That it might not blow through and damage.

As the coldness of my pride and self-righteousness
Blew directly upon others
You tried to temper it by
Removing some of the hurt.

Kindness, you're such a helpful friend.
Why do I neglect you so
And fail to keep you clean and useful?

HEALING IN HIS WINGS . . .

In her tongue is the law of kindness.

PROV. 31:26b

And be ye kind one to another.

EPH. 4:32a

Put on therefore, as the elect of God, holy and beloved, bowels of mercies, kindness, humbleness of mind, meekness, longsuffering;
Forbearing one another, and forgiving one another.
COL. 3:12,13a

And beside this, giving all diligence, add to your faith virtue; and to virtue knowledge;
And to godliness brotherly kindness.

2 PET. 1:5,7a

But in all things approving ourselves as the ministers of God . . . By pureness, by knowledge, by longsuffering, by kindness.

2 COR. 6:4a,6a

Charity suffereth long and is kind.

1 COR. 13:4a

Bitterness

Bitterness, I thought you had gone,
      but I see that you haven't.

The wound itself has almost healed
      but you are the ugly, unsightly
      scar tissue which covers it
Constantly recalling the agony and
      pain I thought I had
      successfully conquered.

I cannot live with you like this
So I shall bring you to Christ
And ask that He help me deal with you
Either as plastic surgeon, removing
      you completely through His
      restoring love
Or as therapist, teaching me to
      rise above you as I view the
      scars of this experience
With new perspective—
      a friendly symbol of spiritual victory.

Healing in His Wings . . .

———•◆•———

*Let all bitterness, and wrath, and anger, and clamour,
and evil speaking, be put away from you, with all malice.*

EPH. 4:31

*Looking diligently lest any man fail of the grace of God;
lest any root of bitterness springing up trouble you, and
thereby many be defiled.*

HEB. 12:15

*In everything by prayer and supplication with thanks-
giving let your requests be made known unto God.*

PHIL. 4:6b

*But the fruit of the spirit is love, joy, peace, longsuffer-
ing, gentleness, goodness, faith, meekness, temperance.*

GAL. 5:22,23a

[71]

Peace

Peace, you are my God-given daily manna
    from heaven.

Humanly, I feel the urge to package you
    to use for my tomorrows
But like God's children in their wilderness
I, too, am learning that you do not keep;
And a fresh supply must be sought
    each day.

So when I feel turmoil and distress within
I realize I've not taken time
To gather a new supply from God
To see me through that day.

HEALING IN HIS WINGS . .

———•—•—•———

Thou wilt keep him in perfect peace, whose mind is stayed on thee: because he trusteth in thee.

ISAIAH 26:3

And the peace of God, which passeth all understanding, shall keep your hearts and minds through Christ Jesus.

PHIL. 4:7

Great peace have they which love thy law: and nothing shall offend them.

PSALM 119:165

These things have I spoken unto you, that in me ye might have peace. In the world ye shall have tribulation: but be of good cheer; I have overcome the world.

JOHN 16:33

Peace I leave with you, my peace I give unto you: not as the world giveth, give I unto you. Let not your heart be troubled, neither let it be afraid.

JOHN 14:27

The work of righteousness shall be peace; and the effect of righteousness quietness and assurance forever.

ISAIAH 32:17

[73]

Compassion

Compassion, how can it be that
    I have not known you personally before?
Can it be that my self-centered heart,
Absorbed only with its own misery,
Was opaque to others' needs?

Then, with your help I reached the second stage
And became translucent
When I grudgingly discovered that some
    others have grief greater than my own.

Stay with me, friend, and help me
    achieve transparency
So that others' woes and needs will come through
    more clearly
And evoke warm sympathy
    and ready help from me.

Healing in His Wings . . .

———•—•—

Finally, be ye all of one mind, having compassion one of another.

1 PETER 3:8a

Bear ye one another's burdens, and so fulfill the law of Christ.

GAL. 6:2

Thus speaketh the Lord of hosts, saying, Execute true judgment, and shew mercy and compassions every man to his brother.

ZECH. 7:9

Blessed are the merciful: for they shall obtain mercy.
MATT. 5:7

What doth the Lord require of thee, but to do justly, and to love mercy, and to walk humbly with thy God?
MICAH 6:8b

Be ye therefore merciful, as your father also is merciful.
LUKE 6:36

Lazarus

Lazarus, you are the silent one!
Why don't you answer my questions
Instead of sitting there like a deaf mute?
What lies beyond the grave?
If you would but assuage my fears!

Your eyes are kind, though,
And your smile shows understanding
And your hand is warm and comforting.
Are you trying to tell me
To trust God's silence too?
That He is near, though quiet,
Tenderly watching to see that all is well?
That my heart could not understand the answers yet
If He should speak just now,
That I must wait 'til He knows my life is ready
        for them?

Then I shall try to humbly wait.

HEALING IN HIS WINGS . . .

Keep not thou silence, O God: hold not thy peace, and be not still, O God.

PSALM 83:1

How long, Lord? wilt thou hide thyself forever?

PSALM 89:46a

My God, my God, why hast thou forsaken me? why art thou so far from helping me, and from the words of my roaring?

O my God, I cry in the daytime, but thou hearest not; and in the night season, and am not silent.

PSALM 22:1,2

Wait on the Lord: be of good courage, and he shall strengthen thine heart: wait, I say, on the Lord.

PSALM 27:14

Hast thou not known? hast thou not heard, that the everlasting God, the Lord, the Creator of the ends of the earth, fainteth not, neither is weary? there is no searching of his understanding.

But they that wait upon the Lord shall renew their strength; they shall mount up with wings as eagles; they shall run, and not be weary; and they shall walk, and not faint.

ISAIAH 40:28,31

God's Word

---•◆•◆•---

God's Word, I see that you are with me still,
Though much of you has been hidden in my heart
    since childhood.

Throughout the years
You've been my daily supplement
Of vitamins and minerals
Helping build up spiritual stamina.

And now in my great time of need when I have been
Weakened by life's onslaught
You have become the glucose
Which helps sustain me
Feeds my soul,
Comforts
    and strengthens me.

HEALING IN HIS WINGS . . .

Trouble and anguish have taken hold on me: yet thy commandments are my delights.

PSALM 119:143

This is my comfort in my affliction: for thy word hath quickened me.

PSALM 119:50

Man doth not live by bread only, but by every word that proceedeth out of the mouth of the Lord doth man live.

DEUT. 8:3b

Lay up his words in thine heart.

JOB 22:22b

Thy word have I hid in mine heart.

PSALM 119:11a

For whatsoever things were written aforetime were written for our learning, that we through patience and comfort of the scriptures might have hope.

ROM. 15:4

The entrance of thy words giveth light; it giveth understanding unto the simple.

PSALM 119:130

[79]

Gratitude

Gratitude, you want to be my
    "constant" companion?
But you bother me—I want to be
    alone and enjoy my
    "persecution."

You say that's how I keep getting
    all these bruises?
That my own antagonism causes me to
    bump into sharp edges
Which you could cushion if I but let you
    walk with me?

Then come along, my friend, and
With your help
I shall try to look more earnestly for
    the good things all about me.

HEALING IN HIS WINGS . . .

———◆•◆•◆———

. . . and be ye thankful.

COL. 3:15b

In everything give thanks.

I THES. 5:18a

Thanks be unto God for his unspeakable gift.

2 COR. 9:15

By him therefore let us offer the sacrifice of praise to God continually, that is, the fruit of our lips giving thanks to his name.

HEB. 13:15

I exhort therefore, that, first of all, supplications, prayers, intercessions, and giving of thanks, be made for all men.

1 TIM. 2:1

O give thanks unto the Lord, for he is good: for his mercy endureth forever.

PSALM 107:1

Be thankful unto him, and bless his name.

PSALM 100:4b

Guilt

Guilt, you bully,
You've found a secret hiding place
In the dark recesses of my mind!

Somehow I've been afraid to really seek you out
For fear you'd win our little game
And I'd forever be the loser.
So, defensive, I've stood at home base,
    guarding it
Lest you steal in.

Now I shall launch the offensive.
I claim God's personal promise of help,
And faith has strengthened my weak knees.

So I shall bravely seek your hiding place
And race you to home plate
Where I shall tag you out forever
With God's forgiving love.

HEALING IN HIS WINGS . . .

He that covereth his sins shall not prosper; but whoso confesseth and forsaketh them shall have mercy.

PROV. 28:13

I sought the Lord, and he heard me, and delivered me from all my fears.

PSALM 34:4

But there is forgiveness with thee.

PSALM 130:4a

He hath not dealt with us after our sins; nor rewarded us according to our iniquities.

For as the heaven is high above the earth, so great is his mercy toward them that fear him.

As far as the east is from the west, so far hath he removed our transgressions from us.

Like as a father pitieth his children, so the Lord pitieth them that fear him.

For he knoweth our frame: he remembereth that we are dust.

PSALM 103:10–14

Failure

———·•••·———

Failure, must you cripple me for life?
You are bound so tightly about my feet
That they have ceased to grow
And now I hobble every painful step through life
Like some little Chinese woman of the distant past.

You say that I have been quite foolish?
That you are momentary and not forever?
That your role is to correct and not to punish?
Help me discern your lessons then:
      My human flaws—God's perfection
      My wavering loyalty—God's faithfulness
      My insufficiency—His adequacy.

And now, O Lord, unbind my weary feet of failure.
Straighten them once more
And free me to walk confidently with Thee
      Into my future.

HEALING IN HIS WINGS . . .

Forgetting those things which are behind, and reaching forth unto those things which are before, I press toward the mark for the prize of the high calling of God in Christ Jesus.

PHIL. 3:13b,14

Let us lay aside every weight and the sin which doth so easily beset us, and let us run with patience the race that is set before us, Looking unto Jesus the author and finisher of our faith.

HEB. 12:1b,2a

Seeing that ye have put off the old man with his deeds; And have put on the new man, which is renewed in knowledge after the image of him that created him.

COL. 3:9b,10

Now unto him that is able to keep you from falling, and to present you faultless before the presence of his glory with exceeding joy.

JUDE 24

And your feet shod with the preparation of the gospel of peace.

EPH. 6:15

Self

As I view the untouched proof
    of my present self
Too honestly captured by the camera
    of life,
I see ugly blemishes of sin and
    selfishness
And feel despicable indeed.

Yet I know God loves me anyway
And sees great potential therein.
So I shall humbly accept myself
And lovingly help Him day by day
Retouch my life—
      Strengthening weak lines of character
      Removing sins of the spirit
      And correcting worldly flaws
So that together we might create a portrait
    of enduring quality.

And as I learn to accept and love
    my "self"
So I shall learn to accept and
    love others also.

Healing in His Wings . . .

Thy hands have made me and fashioned me: give me understanding.

PSALM 119:73a

Behold, thou desirest truth in the inward parts: and in the hidden part thou shalt make me to know wisdom.

PSALM 51:6

Be ye transformed by the renewing of your mind.

ROM. 12:2b

Not that we are sufficient of ourselves to think anything as of ourselves, but our sufficiency is of God.

2 COR. 3:5

If ye fulfil the royal law according to the scripture, Thou shalt love thy neighbor as thyself, ye do well.

JAMES 2:8

Thou shalt love thy neighbor as thyself.

LEV. 19:18b

The Comforter

———• ◆ ◆ •———

You, then, Holy Spirit, are the Comforter
Who has come even as Christ assured.

I floundered in the icy waters
Of grief and despair
But you have tenderly guided me
     Into the warm and gentle
     Gulf Stream of comfort
In whose current I have ceased to struggle
And can safely "ride" to shore
Where I shall settle down again
And adjust to my new world.

Even there, please continue to sustain
With warm, moist breezes
To temper the cold, bitter climate
     of loneliness and grief.

HEALING IN HIS WINGS . . .

Likewise the Spirit also helpeth our infirmities.

ROM. 8:26a

But the Comforter, which is the Holy Ghost, whom the Father will send in my name, he shall teach you all things, and bring all things to your remembrance, whatsoever I have said unto you.

JOHN 14:26

Blessed are they that mourn: for they shall be comforted.

MATT. 5:4

I will not leave you comfortless: I will come to you.

JOHN 14:18

I will never leave thee, nor forsake thee.

HEB. 13:5b

Yea, though I walk through the valley of the shadow of death, I will fear no evil: for thou art with me; thy rod and thy staff they comfort me.

PSALM 23:4

Time

———•◦•———

Hello, Time! I've journeyed far with you
And learned much from the artistry of your wisdom.

I recall when Grief etched stark block prints
    upon my life.
Those lines were sharp and bold
All black and white—clearly defined good and
    evil with no in-between.

But through the years, dear Time, as you have
    walked with me,
In your quiet way
You've lessened the harsh intensity of those lines,
Added a touch of color,
Created depth and perspective.
Working it all together for good, you have
Gently transformed the memory picture
    of that bitter experience
Into a soft watercolor
Much easier to live with day by day.

Welcome, Time—my Artist Friend.

HEALING IN HIS WINGS . . .

When I was a child, I spake as a child, I understood as
a child, I thought as a child: but when I became a man,
I put away childish things.

For now we see through a glass darkly; but then face
to face: now I know in part; but then shall I know even
as also I am known.

1 COR. 13:11,12

Days should speak, and multitude of years should teach
wisdom.

JOB 32:7b

With the ancient is wisdom; and in length of days
understanding.

JOB 12:12

A wise man's heart discerneth both time and judgment.
ECCLES. 8:5b

So teach us to number our days, that we may apply our
hearts unto wisdom.

PSALM 90:12

The Demoniac

How marvelous, Demoniac,
That you are no longer a fragmented being!
Christ was the magnet which drew all parts together
     into a healthy whole.
I understand your great desire
To demonstrate your love
     by going with Him everywhere,
And I know your disappointment when He quietly
     said,
     "Go home and tell."

I'd like so much to be a gleaming rod and reel
Trolling distant waters for my Lord,
But I'm just a simple bamboo pole
Bobbing my cork in the muddy waters
     of everyday living.
Empty of self, though, and pliable to His will,
I can be used to fish for others
     from here on shore
And minister to them in His name.

You say I can also see horizons far beyond,
Can help equip the ones who launch out further
And guide them on their course through prayer?
Thus, even we who stay at home
Can serve Christ everywhere!

[92]

Healing in His Wings . . .

Go home to thy friends, and tell them how great things the Lord hath done for thee, and hath had compassion on thee.

MARK 5:19b

. . . And ye shall be witnesses unto me both in Jerusalem, and in all Judea, and in Samaria, and unto the uttermost part of the earth.

ACTS 1:8b

Ye also helping together by prayer for us . . .

2 COR. 1:11a

Finally, brethren, pray for us, that the word of the Lord may have free course, and be glorified, even as it is with you.

2 THES. 3:1

Go ye therefore, and teach all nations . . . and lo, I am with you always, even unto the end of the world.

MATT. 28:19a, 20b

Inasmuch as ye have done it unto one of the least of these my brethren, ye have done it unto me.

MATT. 25:40b

Christic

Lord Jesus, you are near, for
My soul responds to your presence.
I wear your name, but I'm ashamed;
For my Christian life has been merely
    a weak mixture
In which I've dutifully stirred
    A thimbleful of love
        A cup of morality
           And a pinch of compassion.

Remaining an earthly "mixture" was far easier
Than becoming a heavenly "compound"
      In the crucible of thy will.

No longer am I content to be just a mixture.
I must grow toward spiritual maturity.
Re-apportion Love, Goodness, and Compassion;
Fan into flame my spark of faith,
And in the white heat of thy eternal love,
Remove worldly dross, O Lord,
And transform this weak mixture of self
    Into a dynamic compound,
      Mature Christian,
    With new properties of living,
    Loving, and serving.

Even as I seek to grow, Lord,
Could it be that in thy wondrous grace
Thou canst somehow love and use me
Though only a weak mixture still?

Healing in His Wings . . .

———

Abide in me, and I in you. As the branch cannot bear fruit of itself, except it abide in the vine; no more can ye, except ye abide in me.

JOHN 15:4

Jesus saith unto him, I am the way, the truth, and the life.

JOHN 14:6a

Therefore if any man be in Christ, he is a new creature: old things are passed away; behold, all things are become new.

2 COR. 5:17

They that dwell under his shadows shall return; they shall revive as the corn, and grow as the vine.

HOSEA 14:7a

Unto you that fear my name shall the Sun of righteousness arise with healing in his wings; and ye shall go forth, and grow up.

MALACHI 4:2

. . . Unto you that fear my name shall the Sun of righteousness arise with healing in his wings; and ye shall go forth, and grow up. . .

MALACHI 4:2